May I Quote You, General Grant?

Other volumes in the
The May I Quote You, General . . . ? series

May I Quote You, General Chamberlain?
May I Quote You, General Forrest?
May I Quote You, General Lee? (volume 1)
May I Quote You, General Lee? (volume 2)
May I Quote You, General Longstreet?
May I Quote You, Stonewall Jackson?

MAY I QUOTE YOU, GENERAL GRANT?

Observations and Utterances of the North's Great Generals

Edited by Randall Bedwell

CUMBERLAND HOUSE
NASHVILLE, TENNESSEE

May I Quote You...? is a Registered Trademark of Spiridon Press, Inc.

Some quotes have been edited for clarity and brevity.

Published by Cumberland House Publishing, Inc., 341 Harding Industrial Drive, Nashville, Tennessee 37211.

Managing Editor: Hollis Dodge

Senior Editor: Jimmy Vaden

Contributing Editors: Robert Kerr, Palmer Jones

Research Associate: Jim Fox

Typography: BookSetters

Text design: BookSetters

Library of Congress Cataloging-In-Publication Data

May I quote you, General Grant? : observations and utterances from the   North's greatest generals / edited by Randall Bedwell.

    p. cm. — (May I quote you, General? series)

  ISBN 1-888952-95-4 (pbk. : alk, paper)

  1. Grant, Ulysses S. (Ulysses Simpson), 1822-1885—Quotations. 2. United States—History—Civil War, 1861-1865—Quotations, maxims, etc. 3. Quotations, American, I. Bedwell, Randall J.

E672.1.M36 1998

973.7'092—dc21   98-48024

                                                     CIP

Printed in the United States of America

1 2 3 4 5 6 7 8—02 01 00 99 98

To Rebecca Claxton

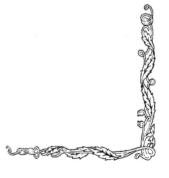

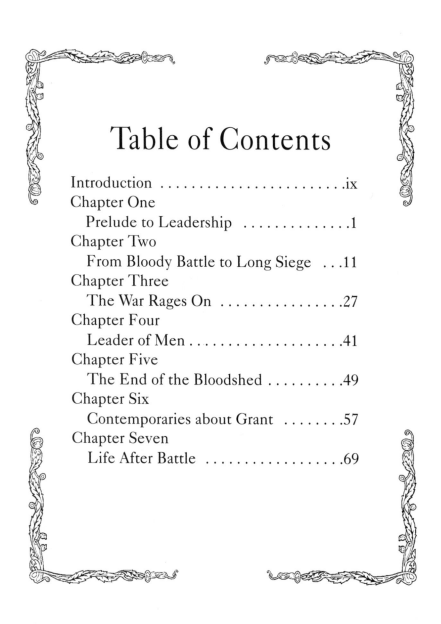

Table of Contents

Introduction ix
Chapter One
    Prelude to Leadership 1
Chapter Two
    From Bloody Battle to Long Siege . . .11
Chapter Three
    The War Rages On 27
Chapter Four
    Leader of Men .41
Chapter Five
    The End of the Bloodshed 49
Chapter Six
    Contemporaries about Grant 57
Chapter Seven
    Life After Battle 69

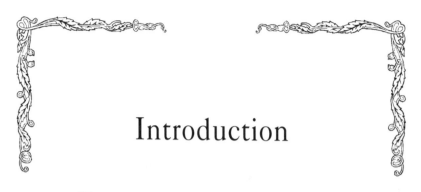

Introduction

His power to wield force to the bitter end . . . .
His concentration of energies, inflexible purpose,
unselfishness, patience, and imperturable long-
suffering, his masterly reticence, ignoring . . .
advice on criticism, his magnanimity in all
relations, but more than all — his infinite trust
in the final triumph of his cause, set him apart
and alone above the others.

—Joshua Lawrence Chamberlain

An unlikely candidate to become a great military leader or President of the United States, Ulysses S. Grant, the son of a Midwestern tanner, accomplished both. His determination

and abilities inspired great loyalty in his officers, troops, and friends, but most of all, in
President Lincoln, who trusted his leadership
to save the Union during the Civil War.

An expert on leadership, Bill Holton, author
of *From Battlefield to Bottom Line*, explains that
"The art of leadership is a painting constantly
in progress. The canvas is the experience; the
colors are the leader's personality, track record,
and credentials; and the brush is synchronicity,
which brings leaders and circumstances
together at precisely the appointed hour."
Ulysses S. Grant brought the canvas, colors, and
brush into perfect harmony for a painting that
carried him through the Civil War and into the
White House.

This unassuming man spoke little, but when
he did, his words were direct, insightful, and
reflected the situation at hand. They also
revealed his modesty, clear thinking, and unwa-

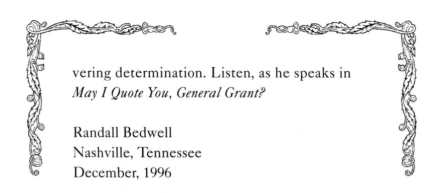

vering determination. Listen, as he speaks in
May I Quote You, General Grant?

Randall Bedwell
Nashville, Tennessee
December, 1996

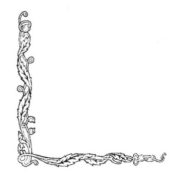
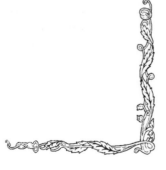

Ulysses S. Grant

CHAPTER ONE

Prelude to Leadership

Besides showing determination to accomplish whatever he pursued, few would have suspected that Hiram Ulysses Grant (later known as Ulysses S.) would be destined for a place in history.

After graduating from West Point—where he discovered a dislike for military discipline, a fondness for horsemanship, and a weakness for liquor (a vice that would haunt him most of his life)—Grant experienced his first military battles in the Mexican War. When the killing commenced, he was ready to resign from the army; however, the excitement of combat helped diminish his fears, and he stepped up to the challenge to become a vital force in the army.

"I have found in Lieutenant Grant a most remarkable and valuable soldier. I anticipate for him a brilliant future if he should have an opportunity to display his powers when they mature," wrote Tom Hamer, Brigadier General of volunteers in the Mexican War. It looked as if Hamer was sorely mistaken when the young lieutenant failed at side businesses, resorted to drinking, and was asked to resign from the army.

In despair, Grant returned to work for his father in Ohio, where he began a fervent study of military strategy. Despite the fact that his past experiences in battle had increased his distaste for bloodshed, when the Civil War began, Grant decided to return to his country's service if they would have him. Perhaps he was not yet a leader, but his determination might lead him in pursuit of high command.

Papa says I
may offer you twenty dollars
for the colt, but if you won't take
that, I am to offer twenty-two and
a half, and if you won't take that,
to give you twenty-five.

*—Grant as an eight-year-old, buying a horse
from a neighbor and showing his lack
of business sense at an early age*

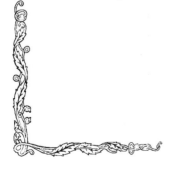

I had a very exalted idea of the acquirements necessary to get through. I did not believe I possessed them, and could not bear the idea of failing.

—on his appointment to West Point

There is no safety from ruin by liquor except by abstaining from it altogether.

I never learned to swear . . . I could never see the use of swearing . . . I have always noticed . . . that swearing helps to rouse a man's anger.

I regard the war as one of the most unjust ever waged by a stronger against a weaker nation. It was an instance of a republic . . . not considering justice in their desire to acquire additional territory.

—*on the Mexican War*

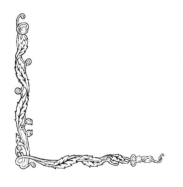

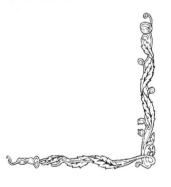

All secret, oath-bound political parties are dangerous to any nation, no matter how pure or how patriotic the motives and principles which first bring them together. . . . [If] a sect sets up its laws as binding above the state laws, wherever the two come in conflict this claim must be resisted and suppressed at whatever cost.

—*on having briefly been a member of the American, or Know-Nothing Party, 1856*

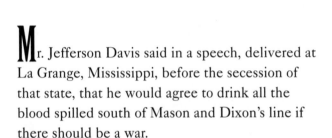

Mr. Jefferson Davis said in a speech, delivered at La Grange, Mississippi, before the secession of that state, that he would agree to drink all the blood spilled south of Mason and Dixon's line if there should be a war.

—from Grant's Memoirs

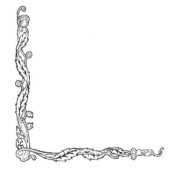

Secession was illogical as well as impracticable; it was revolution.

—on the prelude to the Civil War

The great bulk of the legal voters of the South were men who owned no slaves. . . . Under the old régime they were looked down upon by those who controlled all the affairs in the interest of slave owners, as poor white trash who were allowed the ballot so long as they cast it according to direction.

My own views at that time [1861] were like those officially expressed by [Secretary of State] Seward at a later day, that 'the war would be over in ninety days'. I continued to entertain these views until after the battle Shiloh.

Having served for fifteen years in the regular army . . . I have the honor, very respectfully, to tender my services, until the close of the war, in such capacity as may be offered.

—Grant's petition to be reinstated in
the Union army, May 24, 1861

I see from the papers that my name has been sent in for Brigadier General. This is certainly very complimentary to me particularly as I have never asked a friend to intercede in my behalf. Hearing that I was likely to be promoted, the officers, with great unanimity have requested to be attached to my command. This I don't want you to read to others for I very much dislike speaking of myself.

—from a letter to his father, August 3, 1861

Abraham Lincoln

CHAPTER TWO

From Bloody Battle to Long Siege

Accepted back into the Army's fold, U. S. Grant first commanded the 21st Illinois volunteers and, soon after, took control of federal troops. His men fought valiantly to defend Paducah, gained a victory at the battle of Belmont, and captured Fort Henry and Fort Donelson.

At Shiloh, the Confederates completed a surprise attack on Sherman's men and almost annihilated them. Grant arrived only to find 5,000 frantic

Union soldiers fleeing, abandoned by their commanders who were trying to save themselves. Galloping through the troops, Grant rallied them to turn and fight, holding off the enemy until reinforcements arrived. Grant's strategic studies paid off the following day when the Confederates unexpectedly attacked from the right. He ordered a daring counterattack, forcing the Confederates to fall back. With the loss of 10,000 men on each side, however, the victory was hollow.

Capturing Vicksburg would be an important accomplishment, but the city was strongly fortified by guns facing the Mississippi River.

Positioning troops on the opposite side of the river, Grant determinedly spent four months coping with rains, flooded bayous, and muddy roads before the troops could cross the river, take Jackson, and conquer Vicksburg, which Pemberton finally surrendered after a long and bloody siege. Winning control of the Mississippi made Grant hero of the day and Lincoln's newest major general.

The South had
from thirty to forty percent
of the educated soldiers of the
nation. They had no standing army
and, consequently, these trained
soldiers had to find employment with
the troops from their own states. In
this way what there was of military
education and training was
distributed throughout their
whole army. The whole
loaf was leavened.

*—on the advantage the South possessed over the
North at the beginning of the rebellion*

These positions were of immense importance to the enemy; and of course correspondingly important for us to possess ourselves of.

> —*on Forts Henry and Donelson, situated*
> *about eleven miles apart on the Tennessee*
> *and Cumberland Rivers respectively*

The two positions [Forts Henry and Donelson] were so important to the enemy, as he saw his interest, that it was natural to suppose that reinforcements would come from every quarter from which they could be got. Prompt action on our part was imperative.

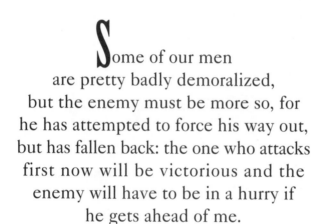

Some of our men
are pretty badly demoralized,
but the enemy must be more so, for
he has attempted to force his way out,
but has fallen back: the one who attacks
first now will be victorious and the
enemy will have to be in a hurry if
he gets ahead of me.

—Fort Donelson, February 15, 1862

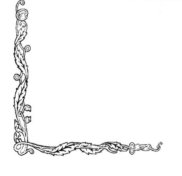

Du/ring the night [Nathan Bedford] Forrest [C.S.A.] also, with his cavalry and some other troops, about a thousand in all, made their way out, passing between our right and the river.

—*Fort Donelson, February 15, 1862*

No terms except an unconditional and immediate surrender can be accepted. I propose to move immediately upon your works.

—*the famous response to General Simon Buckner, when the latter wanted to know what terms of surrender Grant would accept. Grant's nickname, "Unconditional Surrender," derives from this incident, February 16, 1862*

The art of war is simple enough. Find out where your enemy is. Get at him as soon as you can. Strike him as hard as you can, and keep moving on.

Retreat? No. I propose to attack at daylight and whip them.

—Grant at Shiloh, Tennessee, April 6, 1862

I saw an open field . . . so covered with dead that it would have been possible to walk across the clearing, in any direction, stepping on dead bodies, without a foot touching the ground.

—describing the bloody battle at Shiloh, 1862

He was a man of high character and ability . . . the most formidable man . . . that the Confederacy would produce.

> —*on Albert Sidney Johnston,*
> *Grant's opponent at Shiloh*

The distant rear of an army is not the best place from which to judge correctly what is going on in front.

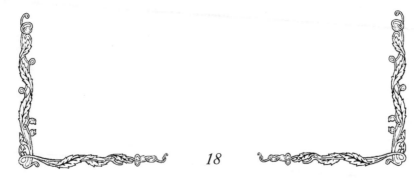

The enemy had fought bravely, but they had started out to defeat and destroy an army and capture a position. They failed in both, with very heavy losses in killed and wounded, and must have gone back discouraged and convinced that the 'yankee' was not an enemy to be despised.

—Shiloh, April 1862

The remainder of the magnificent army of 120,000 men which entered Corinth on the 30th of May had now become so scattered that I was put entirely on the defensive in a territory whose population was hostile to the Union.

—on the occupation of West Tennessee and North Mississippi, July 1862

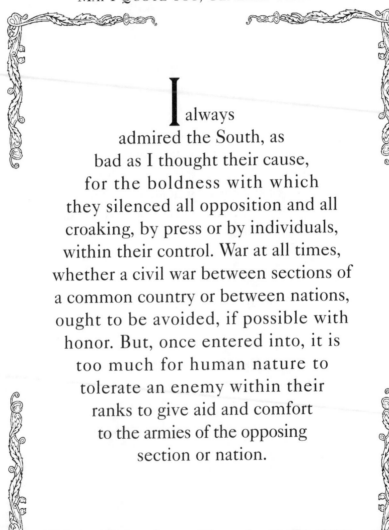

I always
admired the South, as
bad as I thought their cause,
for the boldness with which
they silenced all opposition and all
croaking, by press or by individuals,
within their control. War at all times,
whether a civil war between sections of
a common country or between nations,
ought to be avoided, if possible with
honor. But, once entered into, it is
too much for human nature to
tolerate an enemy within their
ranks to give aid and comfort
to the armies of the opposing
section or nation.

Two commanders on the same field are always one too many.

> —*response to Major General John McClernand,*
> *whom he relieved of command at Young's Point,*
> *prior to the siege of Vicksburg, January 1863*

It was my judgement at the time that to make a backward movement as long as that from Vicksburg to Memphis, would be interpreted . . . as a defeat, and that the draft would be resisted, desertions ensue and the power to capture and punish deserters lost. There was nothing left to be done but to *go forward to a decisive victory.* This was in my mind from the moment I took command in person at Young's Point.

Both the army and navy were so distrustful of [General] McClernand's fitness to command that, while they would do all they could to insure success, this distrust was an element of weakness. It would have been criminal to send troops under these circumstances into such danger.

We are going through a campaign here such as has not been heard of on this continent before.

—during the Vicksburg campaign, March 1863

I now determined upon a regular siege—to 'outcamp the enemy', as it were, and to incur no more losses.

—Vicksburg, April 1863

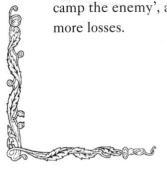

22

Everyone has his superstitions. One of mine is that in positions of great responsibility every one should do his duty to the best of his ability where assigned by competent authority, without application or the use of influence to change his position.

—the maxim Grant relied upon to sustain him during the Vicksburg siege, when many in the North were calling for his removal

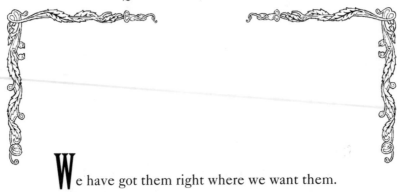

We have got them right where we want them.

—*Vicksburg, 1863*

Men who have shown much endurance and courage as those now in Vicksburg will always challenge the respect of an adversary, and I can assure you will be treated with all the respect due to prisoners of war.

—*Grant to Confederate General John C. Pemberton, Vicksburg, July 3, 1863*

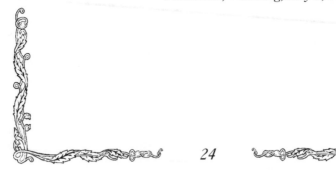

The useless effusion of blood you propose stopping by this course can be ended at any time you choose, by the unconditional surrender of the city and garrison.

—*to General Pemberton, July 3, 1863*

The fate of the Confederacy was sealed when Vicksburg fell. Much hardfighting was to be done afterwards and many precious lives were to be sacrificed; but the morale was with the supporters of the Union ever after.

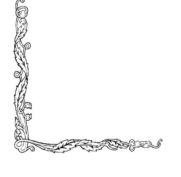

Nathan Bedford Forrest

CHAPTER THREE

The War Rages On

After the two major victories at Shiloh and Vicksburg, Grant and his men broke through to Chattanooga, inspiring the besieged Union troops and gaining a renewed enthusiasm. One officer commented: "We began the campaign the moment he reached the field. Everything was done like music; everything was in harmony."

After Grant received the rank of lieutenant general, rumors built more steadily about making Grant President. He wrote to a friend: "I am not a

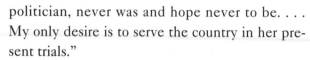

politician, never was and hope never to be. . . . My only desire is to serve the country in her present trials."

To this end, he realized he would have to work at occupying the whole South if he were to defeat Lee. His plan was to wage simultaneous battles around the region while trying to keep the casualties low. Grant believed exhaustion loomed on both sides, so the one that pressed the fighting would be victorious. They fought hard at the battles of the Wilderness, Spotsylvania, Cold Harbor, and Petersburg. Finally they took Richmond, sending the Confederates fleeing. Sheridan's cavalry cut them off at Appomattox Court House, and the South's fate was sealed.

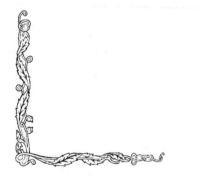
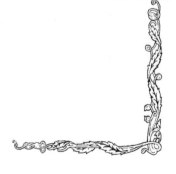

In war, anything is better than indecision. We must decide. If I am wrong we shall soon find it out and can do the other thing. But not to decide wastes both time and money and may ruin everything.

—on the pitfalls of indecision, 1863

I never held a council of war in my life. I heard what men had to say—the stream of talk at headquarters—but I made up my own mind, and from my written orders my staff got their first knowledge of what was to be done. No living man knew of plans until they matured and decided.

There is no great sport in having bullets flying about one in every direction, but I find they have less horror when among them than when in anticipation.

I never had time.

> —*Grant's reply to an officer asking if
> he ever felt fear on the battlefield*

On several occasions during the war [Confederate President Jefferson Davis] came to the relief of the Union army by means of his *superior military genius.*

> —*a sarcastic Grant commenting on the
> high opinion the Southern president had
> of his own capacity for military affairs*

The victory at Chattanooga was won against great odds, considering the advantage the enemy had of position, and was accomplished more easily than was expected by reason of [Confederate General] Bragg's making several grave mistakes.

It would have been a victory for us to have got our army away from Chattanooga safely. It was a manifold greater victory to drive away the besieging army; a still greater one to defeat that army in his chosen ground and nearly annihilate it.

After Chattanooga, following in the same half year with Gettysburg in the East and Vicksburg in the West, there was much the same feeling in the South at this time that there had been in the North the fall and winter before. If the same license had been allowed the people and press in the South that was allowed in the North, Chattanooga would probably have been the last battle fought for the preservation of the Union.

Let us succeed in crushing the rebellion in the shortest possible time, and I will be content with whatever credit may then be given me, feeling assured that a just public will award all that is due.

—December 17, 1863

In time of war the President, being by the Constitution Commander-in-chief of the Army and Navy, is responsible for the selection of commanders. He should not be embarrassed in making his selections.

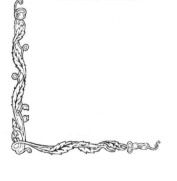

With the aid of the noble armies that have fought in so many fields for our common country, it will be my earnest endeavor not to disappoint your expectations. I feel the full weight of the responsibilities now devolving on me.

—Grant on his appointment to the rank of Lieutenant General, March 9, 1864

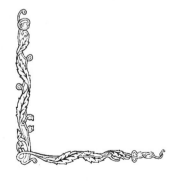
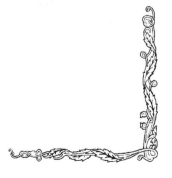

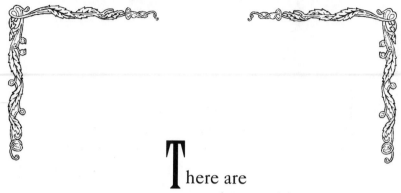

T here are
many men who would
have done better than I did
under the circumstances in which
I found myself. If I had never held
command; if I had fallen, there were
10,000 behind who would have
followed the contest to the end
and never surrendered
the Union.

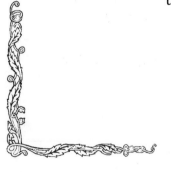

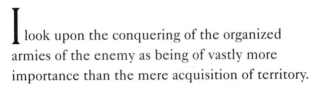

I look upon the conquering of the organized armies of the enemy as being of vastly more importance than the mere acquisition of territory.

> —*to Nathaniel P. Banks, March 15, 1864*

I propose to fight it out on this line if it takes all summer.

> —*Grant at Spotsylvania Court House, May 11, 1864*

I shall take no backward steps.

> —*Grant at Spotsylvania Court House, 1864*

The world has never seen so bloody and so protracted a battle as the one being fought and I hope never will again.

> —*Spotsylvania Court House, 1864*

Well, General, we can't do these little tricks without losses.

—to one of his commanders at Spotsylvania, 1864

I don't believe in strategy in the popular understanding of the term. I use it to get up just as close to the enemy as practicable, with as little loss of life as possible. Then, up guards, and at 'em.

—from a conversation

The striking fact is thus established that we had more men killed and wounded in the first six months of Grant's campaign than Lee had at any one period of it in his whole army. The hammering business had been hard on the hammerer.

—Joshua Lawrence Chamberlain

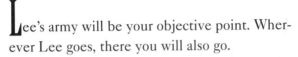

Lee's army will be your objective point. Wherever Lee goes, there you will also go.

—to General George Meade, 1864

Oh, I am heartily tired of hearing about what Lee is going to do. Some of you always seem to think he is suddenly going to turn a double somersault and land in our rear and on both of our flanks at the same time. Go back to your command, and try to think what we are going to do ourselves, instead of what Lee is going to do.

—to his officers at the Wilderness, May 1864

If you see the President, tell him from me that whatever happens there will be no turning back.

*—to journalist Henry Wing after
the battle of the Wilderness*

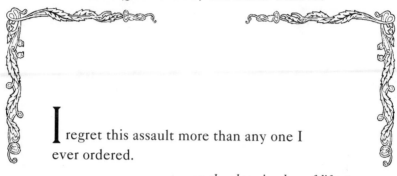

I regret this assault more than any one I ever ordered.

*—on the alarming loss of life at
Cold Harbor, June 3, 1864*

This army has now won a most decisive victory and followed the enemy. That is all it ever wanted — to make as good an army as ever fought a battle.

*—to Sherman on the breaking of Lee's
lines at Petersburg, April 3, 1865*

It now became a life and death struggle with Lee to get south.

—on Lee's retreat from Petersburg, April 1865

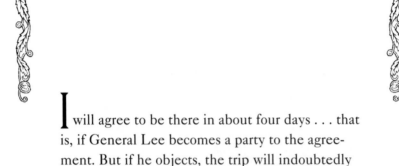

I will agree to be there in about four days . . . that is, if General Lee becomes a party to the agreement. But if he objects, the trip will indoubtedly be prolonged.

> —*Grant, in response to a reporter's question as to how long it will take to reach Richmond, 1864*

It is possible that the Southern man started in with a little more dash than his Northern brother, but he was correspondingly less enduring.

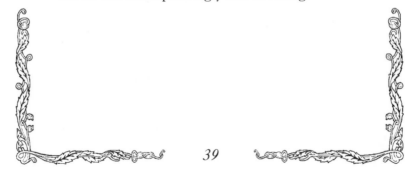

George B. McClellan

CHAPTER FOUR

Leader of Men

Ulysses S. Grant inspired the respect of his Union troops. As Horace Porter stated: "His soldiers always knew that he was ready to rough it with them and share their hardships on the march. He wore no better clothes than they, and often ate no better food." Instead of a handsome general's uniform, Grant wore the plain uniform of a private, only with three stars on his shoulder. His generals dismissed his modesty as one of his eccentricities. They laughed about his breakfasts

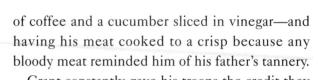

of coffee and a cucumber sliced in vinegar—and having his meat cooked to a crisp because any bloody meat reminded him of his father's tannery.

Grant constantly gave his troops the credit they deserved. At Shiloh he understandingly forgave the Union troops who had panicked while their commanders fled to save themselves. In the battle for Vicksburg, some of the Union defenders were African-American regiments. Fighting valiantly, they repelled an assault from the Confederates, which Grant proudly reported to Lincoln.

Cheers for Grant were cheers for his men's own triumph over misfortune. Those who fought and died for Grant believed they shared a part of his glory, a glint of his success, when they gave up their lives.

I feel every confidence of success, and the best feeling prevails among the men.

—Grant to Halleck, Fort Donelson,
February 12, 1862

Better troops never went on a battlefield.

—Grant on the Union troops
who had panicked at Shiloh

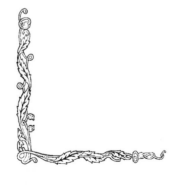
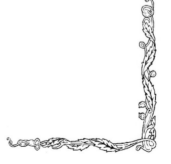

There is one thing I feel well assured of, that is, that I have the confidence of every brave man in my command.

—after Shiloh, April 26, 1862

The men have fought this war, and the men will finish it.

—March 1865

Experience proves that the man who obstructs a war in which his nation is engaged, no matter whether right or wrong, occupies no enviable place in life or history.

The most favorable posthumous history the stay-at-home traitor can hope for is oblivion.

I have known a few men who were always aching for a fight when there was no enemy near, who were as good as their word when the battle did come. But the number of such men is small.

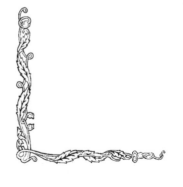
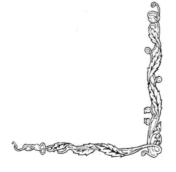

The fact is, troops who have fought a few battles and won, and followed up their victories, improve upon what they were before to an extent that can hardly be counted by percentage. The difference in result is often decisive victory instead of inglorious defeat.

It is men who wait to be selected and not those who seek, from whom we may always expect the most efficient service.

Drill and discipline are worth more to our men than fortifications.

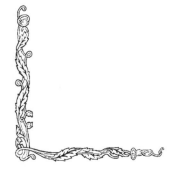
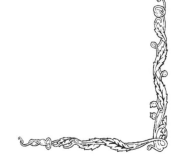

Robert E. Lee

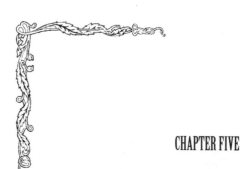
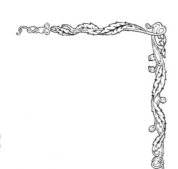

CHAPTER FIVE

The End of Bloodshed

On April 9, 1865, General Ulysses S. Grant, dressed in rough clothing, and General Robert E. Lee, outfitted in full uniform, met at a two-story farmhouse in Appomattox Court House, Virginia. After a handshake and a cordial discussion, the two military leaders set forth the terms for the surrender of the Army of Northern Virginia: Officers and soldiers were to be disarmed, placed on parole, and forbidden to take up arms again against the Union. To Lee's delight, the officers were permitted to

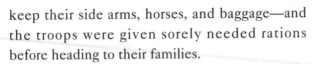

keep their side arms, horses, and baggage—and the troops were given sorely needed rations before heading to their families.

This meeting culminated a four-year civil war that saw the tragic death of some 600,000 young Americans. Grant remarked, "This war was a fearful lesson, and should teach us the necessity of avoiding wars in the future." The South's defeat marked the beginning of the end to slavery in the country and established supremacy of federal over states' rights, keeping Americans as one nation between Canada and Mexico.

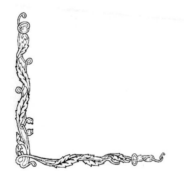
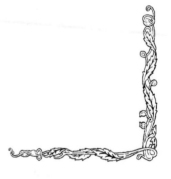

We wished to see everything of the opposing army, now that it had become civil enough for the first time in its existence to let us get close up to it. The general, however had no desire to look at the conquered—indeed, he had little curiosity in his nature.

—Horace Porter on Grant, Appomattox
Court House, 1865

The war is over. The rebels are our countrymen again.

—Grant at Appomattox Court House

I felt sad and depressed at the downfall of a foe who had fought so long and valiantly, and suffered so much for a cause, though the cause was, I believe, one of the worst for which a people ever fought.

—*on Robert E. Lee at Appomattox Court House*

As he was a man of much dignity, with an impassable face, it was impossible to say whether he felt inwardly glad that the end had finally come, or felt sad over the result, and was too manly to show it.

—*on Robert E. Lee at Appomattox Court House*

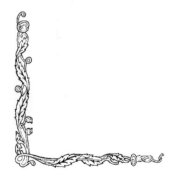
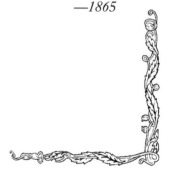

There was not a man in the whole Confederacy whose influences with the soldierly and the whole people were as great as his.

—on Robert E. Lee

The suffering that must exist in the South . . . will be beyond conception; people who speak of further retaliation and punishment do not conceive of the suffering endured already, or are heartless and unfeeling.

—1865

There was no time during the rebellion when I did not think, and after say, that the South was more to be benefited by its defeat than the North. . . . The war was expensive to the South as well as to the North, both in blood and treasure, but it was worth all the cost.

The Southern rebellion was largely an outgrowth of the Mexican war. Nations, like individuals, are punished for their transgressions. We got our punishment in the most sanguinary and expensive wars of modern times.

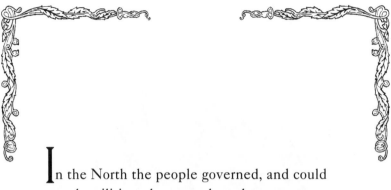

In the North the people governed, and could stop hostilities whenever they chose to stop supplies. The South was a military camp, controlled absolutely by the government with soldiers to back it, and the war could have been protracted, no matter to what extent the discontent reached, up to the point of open mutiny of the soldiers themselves.

Ifs" defeated the Confederates.

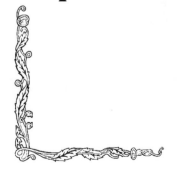

William T. Sherman

CHAPTER SIX

Contemporaries on Grant

Although he was not loved by everyone, especially one of his commanders—General Henry Halleck—who thwarted his actions at every turn, he gained the admiration of officers and subordinates on both sides of the battlefield.

Union General George Meade commented, "Grant is not a mighty genius but he is a good soldier with a great force of character, honest and upright, of pure purposes. Take him all in, he is in my judgment the best man the war has yet produced."

With each passing battle, Grant gained the confidence and utmost respect of President Lincoln: "I wish to express my entire satisfaction with what you have done up to this time, so far as I understand it. . . . You are vigilant and self-reliant. . . . If there is anything wanting which is within my power to give, do not fail to let me know it. And now with a brave Army, and a just cause, may God sustain you."

And although the battles were long and the losses heavy, Robert E. Lee held no grudges against Grant. He defended his honor as he would any Confederate officer he respected. When a member of his board at Washington College spoke poorly of Grant, Lee retorted: "Sir, if you ever again presume to speak disrespectfully of General Grant in my presence, either you or I will sever his connection with this university."

I can't spare this man—he fights.

—President Abraham Lincoln on Grant, 1862

None who had known him the previous years could recognize him as being the same man. . . . From this time his genius and his energies seemed to burst forth with new life.

—Anonymous Union officer on Grant, May 1863

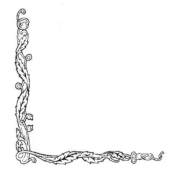

General Grant has full and absolute authority to enforce his own commands. . . . He had the full confidence of the Government, is expected to enforce his authority, and will be firmly and heartily supported.

—*Edwin M. Stanton, Secretary of War, 1863*

Until you had won at Donelson, I confess I was cowed by the terrible array of anarchical elements that presented themselves at every point; but that victory admitted the ray of light which I have followed ever since.

—*General William T. Sherman to Grant, 1864*

Grant's whole character was a mystery to even himself—a combination of strength and weakness not paralleled by any of whom I have read in Ancient or Modern History.

—General Sherman, after the war

He was always amid excitement, and patient under trials. He looked neither to the past with regret nor to the future with apprehension. What he could not control, he endured.

—General Horace Porter on Grant

As for Grant, he was like Thor, the hammerer; striking blow after blow, intent on his purpose to beat his way through, somewhat reckless of the cost.

—*General Joshua Lawrence Chamberlain*

He had somehow, with all his modesty, the rare faculty of controlling his superiors as well as his subordinates. He outfaced Stanton, captivated the President, and even compelled the acquiescence or silence from that dread source of paralyzing power—the Congressional Committee on the Conduct of war.

—*General Joshua Lawrence Chamberlain on Grant*

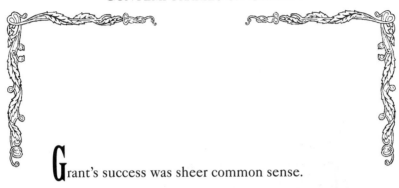

Grant's success was sheer common sense.

—*Confederate General Joseph Johnston*

Grant always seemed pretty certain to win when he went into a fight with anything like equal numbers. I believe the chief reason why he was more successful than others was that while they were thinking so much about what the enemy was going to do, Grant was thinking all the time what he was going to do.

—*General Horace Porter*

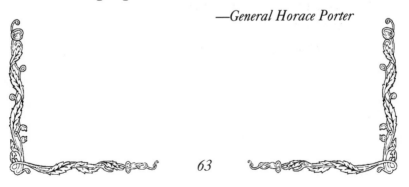

He depended for his success more upon the powers of invention than of adaptation.

—*General Horace Porter on Grant*

There was a spur on the heel of every order [Grant] sent, and his subordinated were made to realize that in battle it is the minutes that control events.

—*General Horace Porter*

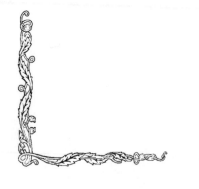
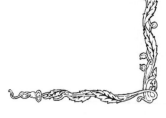

Grant is my man, and I am his the rest of the war.

—*President Lincoln, July 5, 1863*

Why do men fight who were born to be brothers?

—*James Longstreet after meeting his old friend*
Grant at Appomattox, April 9, 1865

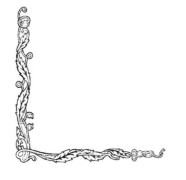
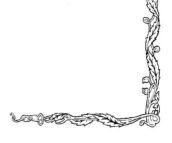

As to Grant's grit and determination, all his predecessors together did not possess as much of these manly qualities.

—*Major Robert Stiles, Army of Northern Virginia*

That man will fight us every day and every hour till the end of the war.

—*James Longstreet speaking of Grant, 1864*

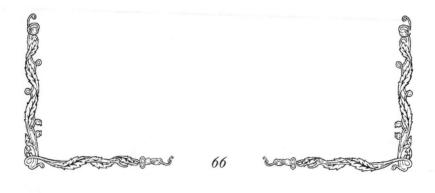

This is the simple soldier, who, all untaught of the silken phrase-makers, linked words together with an art surpassing the art of the schools and put into them a something which will still bring to American ears, as long as America shall last, the roll of his vanished drums and the tread of his marching hosts.

—*Mark Twain*
describing Grant in 1866

David Glasgow Farragut

CHAPTER SEVEN

Life After Battle

Grant's leadership continued off the battlefield. He was hailed a hero by Lincoln after the war and was scheduled to accompany him to Ford Theater on that tragic historical night. His life might have ended with Lincoln's that evening, but his refusal of the invitation showed that fate had other plans for the mighty leader. He was drafted by the Republican party as their candidate for President, seeing him as a person they could probably manipulate for their own profit. Although bored

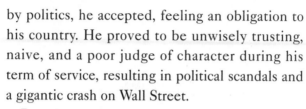

by politics, he accepted, feeling an obligation to his country. He proved to be unwisely trusting, naive, and a poor judge of character during his term of service, resulting in political scandals and a gigantic crash on Wall Street.

Despite this lack of success, Grant was re-elected to a second term by those who refused to abandon their views of him as a war hero. More financial troubles followed and the longest depression the nation had ever known. He left after his second term with a sincere apology to his nation.

After traveling the world, he returned to his mansion in New York City. Despite the pain caused by cancer, he finished his memoirs just before completing his own surrender. The leader of war time and peace time passed away in the summer of 1885.

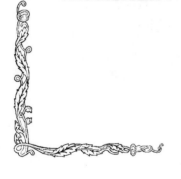

The people
who had been in rebellion
must necessarily come back into
the Union, and be incorporated as an
integral part of the nation. Naturally
the nearer they were placed to an equality
with the people who had not rebelled,
the more reconciled they would feel
with their old antagonists, and the
better citizens they would be from
the beginning. They surely would
not make good citizens if they
felt that they had a yoke
around their necks.

—*Grant after the war*

I would not distress these people. They are feeling their defeat bitterly, and you would not add to it by my witnessing their despair, would you?

> *—to his wife, when she asked if he would*
> *make an appearance in Richmond.*

It has been my misfortune to be engaged in more battles than any other general on the other side of the Atlantic; but there was never a time during my command when I would not have chosen some settlement by reason rather than the sword.

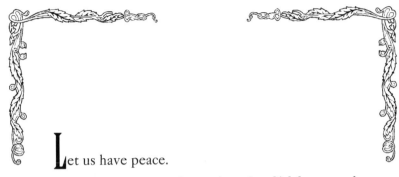

Let us have peace.

> *—from a letter in which he accepted
> the nomination for the presidency.*

If chosen to fill the high office for which you have selected me, I will give to its duties the same energy, the same spirit and the same will that I have given to the performance of all duties which have devolved upon me heretofore. Whether I shall be able to perform these duties to your entire satisfaction time will determine.

> *—as he was nominated*

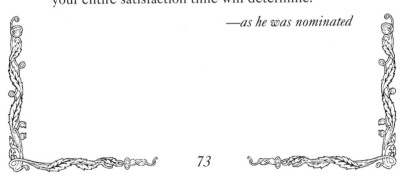

The responsibilities of the position I feel, but accept them without fear.

—when he was elected

I shall have no policy of my own to interfere against the will of the people.

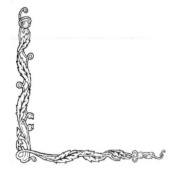
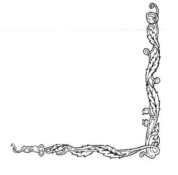

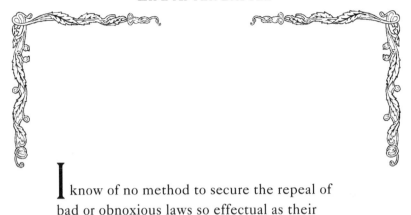

I know of no method to secure the repeal of bad or obnoxious laws so effectual as their strict construction.

Let no guilty man escape, if it can be avoided. No personal considerations should stand in the way of performing a duty.

—endorsement of a letter relating to the
Whiskey Ring scandal, July 29, 1875

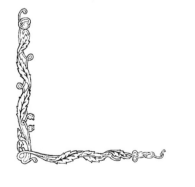

I have acted in every instance from a conscientious desire to do what was right, constitutional, within the law, and for the very best interests of the whole people. Failures have been errors of judgment, not of intent. at the end of his second term.

No American has carried greater fame out of the White House than this silent man who leaves it today.

—*James A. Garfield about President Grant, 1877*

The one thing I never want to see again is a military parade. When I resigned from the army and went to a farm I was happy. When the rebellion came, I returned to the service because it was a duty. I had no thought of rank; all I did was try and make myself useful.

—from a conversation with the Duke of Cambridge

Although a soldier by profession, I have never felt any sort of fondness for war, and I have never advocated it, except as a means of peace.

—from a speech in London

I appreciate the fact, and am proud of it, that the attentions I am receiving are intended more for our country than for me personally.

—letter from London to G.W. Childs, June 1877

I am not egotist enough to suppose all this significance should be given because I was the object of it.

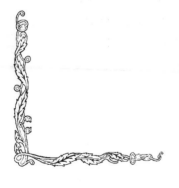
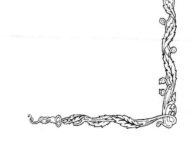

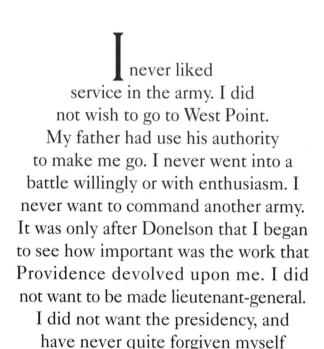

I never liked service in the army. I did not wish to go to West Point. My father had use his authority to make me go. I never went into a battle willingly or with enthusiasm. I never want to command another army. It was only after Donelson that I began to see how important was the work that Providence devolved upon me. I did not want to be made lieutenant-general. I did not want the presidency, and have never quite forgiven myself for resigning the command of the army to accept it.

The fact is I think I am a verb instead of a personal pronoun. A verb is anything that signifies to be, to do, or to suffer. I signify all three.

> —*Grant speaking to his doctor*
> *near the end of his life, 1885*

This is the greatest interest in life, to see my work done.

> —*commenting on his memoirs, 1885*

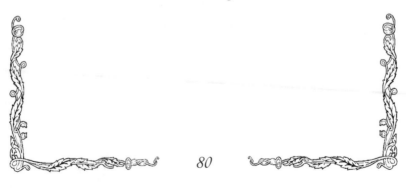

There is nothing more I should do now, and therefore I am not likely to be more ready to go than at this moment.

—on the completion of his memoirs at the approach of his death, 1885

There are but few events in the affairs of men brought about by their own choice.

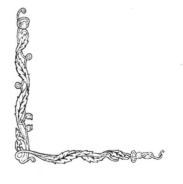
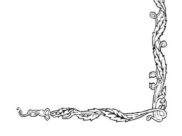

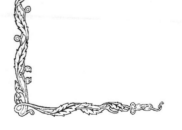

The war has made us a nation of great power and intelligence. We have but little to do to preserve peace, happiness and prosperity at home, and the respect of other nations. Our experience ought to teach us the necessity of the first; our power secures the latter.

—Grant on the Civil War

My experience has taught me two lessons; first, that things are seen plainer after the events have occurred; second, that the most confident critics are generally those who know the least about the matter criticized.

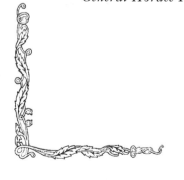

General Grant . . .
and the President . . . served
the country with hearts too great for
rivalry, with souls untouched by jeal-
ousy, and lived to teach the world
that it is time to abandon the path of
ambition when it becomes so narrow
that two cannot walk it abreast.

—*General Horace Porter on Grant and Lincoln*